CRAZY WORLD, PEACEFUL HEART

6 Core Practices for Cultivating Joy and Resilience

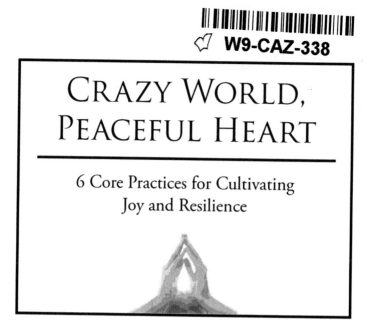

Praise for Sharon Rosen and *Crazy World, Peaceful Heart:*

"This is a small book filled with Big Grace. I am especially inspired by its down-to-earth quality, since I know that "down-to-earth" is the best road to Heaven. May this sweet and wise book of healing find a home in many hearts!"

~ Jinen Jason Shulman, author of Kabbalistic Healing; The Instruction Manual for Receiving God; and founder of A Society of Souls School for Non-Dual healing.

"This beautifully written book wraps its arms around you like a comforting, wise mother. You'll feel calmer just reading it; however it also offers a variety of simple and practical activities to help you recapture a sense of peace in this hectic world in which we live. Sharon's approach is down-to-earth and spiritual at the same time, acknowledging the realities of life while also reminding us that just because the world is crazy doesn't mean we have to be, too."

~ Debbie LaChusa, author of Breaking the Spell: The Truth About Money, Success, and the Pursuit of Happiness

"In *Crazy World, Peaceful Heart,* Sharon Rosen distills wit & wisdom that actually work. She shows, from experience and deep inquiry, how we can weave difficulty and challenge into the fabric of a wise, compassionate life. There are numerous gems here — why we forget to practice what we know is good for us, how to cultivate joy and resilience every mundane day, and so much more. And a bonus — for this pragmatic, non-Jewish creative, I found an inviting doorway to the Kabbalah's wisdom."

~ Jeffrey Davis, Writer & Creativity Consultant, author of The Journey From The Center To The Page

"*Crazy World, Peaceful Heart* inspires you with accessible wisdom and tools to befriend your body, mind, and spirit. Sharon Rosen's healing muse is a precious gift to your life."

~ *Laura Alden Kamm, author of Intuitive Wellness*

"Sharon Rosen's *Crazy World, Peaceful Heart* is a generous guide to the ways of wisdom — from the most challenging like Kabbalah, to the most accessible like breathing as deeply as we can. From the most basic of principles like moving daily and with intention, to the quest to understand gratitude at its deepest level, Sharon takes our minds, hearts and hands and leads us toward how we can learn what we don't know, and to remember what we forgot that we once knew. Hers is a gentle knowing that is deep and not dogmatic. Her voice encourages even as she knows full well how easily we falter. And the peaceful heart she promises is there within us to be found following her basic paths to joy through resilience."

~ *Frances Bartkowski, author of Kissing Cousins:*
A New Kinship Bestiary

"Sharon helps us find the simple (but not easy) solutions in everyday life for building a resilient spirit. She beautifully weaves rich spiritual wisdom and exercises while expressing authentic feelings about life in this complex universe. She has provided us with a powerful life guide of daily principles. I felt blessed and uplifted as I read every word."

~ *Bonnie Berke, Certified Holistic Health Counselor*

CRAZY WORLD, PEACEFUL HEART

6 Core Practices for Cultivating Joy and Resilience

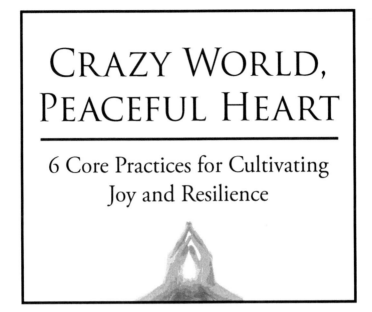

Sharon Helene Rosen

BALBOA
PRESS
A DIVISION OF HAY HOUSE

ISBN: 978-1-4525-5005-3 (sc)
ISBN: 978-1-4525-5006-0 (e)
Library of Congress Control Number: 2012906369
Balboa Press books may be ordered through booksellers or by contacting:

Balboa Press
A Division of Hay House
1663 Liberty Drive
Bloomington, IN 47403
www.balboapress.com
1-(877) 407-4847

Contents

To each of us walking this human path; may we be blessed with peace of mind in these troubled times. Remember:

It's not about perfection.
It's about awareness, and acceptance.
It's about living the full expression
of humanity that you are,
in all of your glory, all of your foolishness,
and all of your complexity,
with honesty and compassion.

INTRODUCTION:

Can't Stop The World

I gave up looking for a reason
To live with things just the way they were...
Can't stop the world, can't stop the world,
can't stop the world, don't let it stop you.

Go-Go's, *Beauty and the Beat*

❧

This is a book about life. It's about the big, messy sprawl of it, "the full catastrophe" as described by fictional philosopher Zorba the Greek. It's about how to live in the reality of this rollicking ride — the pain, the loss, the triumphs, the joys — with your soul intact and thriving. Not because you somehow managed to transcend it all, but because you learned what you need to do to sit in the center of your life and not implode.

I want to share with you the idea that what it takes to maintain a peaceful heart in a crazy world is simple but not necessarily easy. Simple in that the steps themselves are not especially exotic or out of reach: not easy because engaging in them doesn't always come naturally and takes a certain degree of introspection and effort. If you are reading this, then I know that introspection is something you are comfortable with; it's the effort part that has perhaps been more of a bumpy ride!

My own journey was quite bumpy for a long time. Although my earliest sense of myself is of being a happy and confident child (if Mom lost track of me during an outing, *I* wasn't lost, she just couldn't see me), I grew up in a family that was prone to depression on both sides. Some of it was biochemical — there was serious mental illness in my father's family — and some of it was generational. After all, we are Jews, one of the more enduringly persecuted people on earth. And I was born in the late 1950's to parents who came out of the Great Depression, experienced the aftermath of the Nazi regime and World War II, and carried the echo of all of that into our home life.

My own bouts of struggling with depression as a teen and young adult easily gave way to thinking I was doomed, that it was a set point to which I was naturally wired. Along with the tribal/ancestral connection, my grandfather had been hospitalized on several occasions, given shock treatments and mind zoning meds. I had seen my father sit in near silence for days on end, and felt the heavy energy permeating our whole house. And I knew the history of my mother's intense post-partum depression after giving birth to me had nearly cost her her life, and witnessed her recurring bouts with it over the years.

Yet I also experienced extended times of tremendous joy, creativity, connection and lightness, so I knew what was possible. High school introduced me to the social sciences, and I found a true affinity for any "-ology" that explored human development and the intricacies of relationship with self and others. And I always felt a deep inner connection to the Divine. So, set loose into the world after obtaining a BA and deciding not to become a teacher as I'd always imagined, my twenties and thirties were a time of deep introspection. I explored psychological and spiritual teachings from many sources, immersing myself in books, meditation classes and large-scale personal growth workshops such as Actualizations and The Forum. (And yes, I do believe I "got it." Then I lost it again for a while.)

After floundering through a few unsatisfying jobs, I stumbled onto a life path I never could have envisioned. My interest in massage and natural healing, spurred by some chronic health issues that doctors had no help for except pharmaceuticals, led me to a six-month course of study in shiatsu. It began as what I thought was simply a personal quest for healing and growth. I was actually so scared of the commitment involved in enrolling at a massage school, I chose that program partly because it was a one-on-one apprenticeship that I could pay for week by week rather than in one lump sum! If it didn't suit me, well, I could walk away just having paid for whatever knowledge I had gathered. Little did I know when I arrived for my first class that it would lead to a 25-year career as a massage therapist, energy healer and holistic living guide.

Still, my movement on this healing path often felt like a journey of one step forward, two steps back (or more). There was all of that history to overcome. There was the genetics, and then the realization that spending a weekend in a transformational workshop, wonderful and enlightening as it was, didn't necessarily mean that my whole life was transformed. It was more like "just when I thought I was becoming enlightened, I called my mother."

So I continued digesting and synthesizing everything I was learning and studying, eventually finding my way to an intensive four-year training in Kabbalistic Healing. In Kabbalah, I found the unifying themes that I had always felt in my bones and my heart. As a very young girl, I would go to Saturday morning services at our synagogue and feel deeply connected to God through the sounds of the Hebrew prayers and their ancient melodies. But when I would read the English translations of the prayers, I'd go blank—so many words, so much repetition, so much about good or bad, right or wrong, divisiveness and blame!

My inner experience was marked by a feeling of oneness, not duality. Those moments of connection sparked a desire to heal the parts of me that felt wounded by difficult life experiences and expressed those wounds as separation — from other people, from God and even from myself — and to live more from a recognition of the truth that I am always connected to my Source. Kabbalah gave me a unified theory and awakened a sense of wholeness that now weaves through my life and my work.

It is not my intention for this book to teach you about Kabbalah per se, which is beyond the scope of this small volume. But I want to share some key concepts from what I have learned, because I believe they will strengthen both the fabric of my words and your understanding of what it truly takes to have more peace in your heart.

Lessons From The Tribe

Kabbalah means "to receive" and is the core of the Jewish mystical tradition of wisdom received through years of deep study and prayer. For centuries it was shrouded in secrecy by Orthodox men, but in recent decades wise teachers have brought forth its teachings for those who crave spiritual knowledge and a deeper understanding of how life works. Kabbalah provides us with an elegant blueprint for how the universe came into being. It shows us that creation is an ongoing process and we are here to serve and co-create our world with the ultimate Creator.

I was fascinated to learn that the very first letter in Genesis, the first book of the Torah, is beyt, which is the second letter of the Hebrew alphabet. This is because the first letter of the Hebrew alphabet has no true sound, and is understood to be the energy with which God "spoke" the world into being. And that first Hebrew word in Genesis, bereishete, in its most literal translation means "with beginningness" rather than the usual "in the beginning."

This unique wording helps us to understand a couple of things. One, and perhaps most important of all, is that creation did not happen in one moment long ago — "in the beginning." By making it a verb rather than a noun, "with beginningness" helps us to remember that creation is happening in every moment, and we are active participants in the process.

It also helps us to remember that without God, or however you define the Ultimate Source of Creation, nothing comes into being. So we are necessary as much as God is necessary for creation to happen. Or, as my Kabbalah teacher said the first time I met him, "All healing — making whole — happens in relationship." And all wholeness must by definition contain both the light and the dark, held in balance and mercy.

These are tender and mercurial times. The ability to nurture and maintain a peaceful heart is perhaps the most sought after, elusive and mystifying human quest. Part of the problem is that we hope one day to finally arrive at that place — after enough meditations, workshops and effort — and then stay there. The basic dilemma is that *it simply doesn't work that way.* Even the most enlightened master will cry when his child dies, or feel anger when he witnesses evil in action. It is the ability to hold all of it — to feel fully yet not hold tightly — that is the true sign of a peaceful heart.

The steps you take to develop this level of resilience do more than serve you personally as you deal with the ups and downs of your own life. Another key tenet from Judaism that guides and sustains me is called *tikkun olam,* repairing the world. That means with each interaction where you are not adding to the difficulties of the world, you are adding to the healing and restoration of the world. When you focus on strengthening your ability to flow more gracefully with the vicissitudes of life, you are doing more than just helping yourself to feel calm and centered; you are showing up in your life in ways that help others to respond differently to their own stresses and problems as well. As one writer put it:

> Tikkun olam places our spiritual practice at the heart of the epic, unfolding history of the universe: the evolution and spiritualization of the whole of creation. With each small act of kindness, with

each moment of presence and practice, with each effort to see, cleanse, and integrate our inner life, with each heartfelt prayer opening to the higher energies and the higher will, we build the new world and serve the Divine Architect of meaning.
(Joseph Naft, InnerFrontier.org)

So please, take exquisite care of yourself...it's actually for the highest good of all beings and our planet that you do! Especially when it is done with *kavannah*, which translates as "direction of the heart." When your actions are guided by your kavannah — the intention and consciousness that comes from the inherent wisdom of your heart — taking time each day to cultivate joy and resilience goes beyond any whisper of selfishness, and becomes the stuff of universal healing.

Many Paths, One Destination

What you will find in these pages is an exploration of practices that have nurtured and supported me and the many clients with whom I have shared them. They will help you engage in the ongoing work of cultivating inner resilience, moving again and again from the confusion of the head to the wisdom of the heart and body. This is not a step-by-step system that needs to be followed in order, one piece before another. Each practice has an ability to shift and heal you, bringing you back into relationship with your most essential self.

I have found that "what works" changes depending on where I am in the moment, and it's taken me a long time to allow that to be OK. So many books and teachings have 'their way' and focus on the importance of sticking to one way and going deep with it. There is the "sit totally still and don't so much as scratch your nose" form, the "follow your breath in every moment and allow all thoughts to pass through like clouds" form, the "move and sweat and shake it out till you drop" form; all offer a sincere and dedicated path to remembering our connection to the Divine.

But just as there are some mornings when focusing on my breath or a mantra is enough and I can go with and stay with that, there are just as many when it's simply not working. My mind is racing, my heart is twisted with anxiety, and I'm just too antsy or enervated to still myself easily.

This is when I will turn to either chanting or movement to bring myself back to my knowing — the knowing in my body, the body which houses my heart and my spirit. Using my voice, feeling the shapes of the words in my mouth and the vibration of the notes in my cells, grounds me in the moment and opens me to the ever present truth of my connection with my Source.

Allowing myself to dance in my seat, or stand, sway and stretch in whatever way brings a sense of alive presence, helps me to realize that silence and meditation are not the only or best conduits to consciousness.

Or some days the opposite is true — there has been so much motion and purposeful action that I long to simply sit and breathe and become still as I connect to my heart. This is when I remember what I know by following the flow of my breath as it moves through my body, or placing one hand on my heart and chanting a name of God over and over again, till nothing else exists.

☙ **What helps you feel connected to yourself, even if you don't think of it as spiritual or special?**

☙ **What have you learned from teachers along the way that truly resonates and helps you to source the Divine in a real and intimate way?**

☙ **What practices give you the greatest sense of joy and freedom from conflict?**

These are questions to keep in mind as you make your way through these pages.

In Chapter One, you will learn about why balance always has to include difficulty, and how to not use that as an excuse to shut down or give up. You will be introduced to The Basics and why the simplest steps are the most essential ones to master.

The rest of the chapters lay out specific practices that are each designed to help you connect with yourself on a soul level. Some are as natural as breathing; others help you tap into your creativity and self-nurturance. Some involve sitting still and others invite you to move your body and reconnect with its natural rhythms.

Read through the chapters and then feel free to use whatever you are most drawn to as your entry point. It is helpful to have a journal and pen handy so you can make note of insights, go deeper into what may arise as you try different practices, or answer questions posed within the text like those listed above.

You may want to focus on a particular area, like movement or inquiry, and go deeply with that over the course of several weeks. Or you might work with one practice per day for a while and cycle through as your guidance compels you. There is no one right or perfect way to approach the work of finding your resilient center and connecting to your joy. My job is to point out the blazes on the trail; the steps you take upon it are your own.

Steps Make The Path

There is much to be done
  there is much to be done
Saying it twice illuminates
  just how much and how true.

Cast a circle around you and make
    one clear prayer
Watch steam rise from
  your teacup and know that
     everything
  is alive with magic.

Begin here.
Each next step
  will present itself
   unendingly...

SHR ©1994

CHAPTER ONE

What You Once Knew

I forget to remember that I know what I know...

❧

So let's begin at the beginning. Once upon a time you were a baby crawling on the floor. You came upon a fallen raisin, picked it up in your not-too-agile fingers, and most likely put it in your mouth. Ooohhh, sweet! Chewy... dense...sticky...gone! Then the colors of a plant on the windowsill drew your attention. Off you shuffled until you got to a place where you could reach out and pull yourself up to standing, motivated by a pure desire to touch the green leaves — *soft* — and purple blossoms — *softer and strong smelling.*

Years have passed and now you are a woman (or man) at work, sitting in front of a computer, holding a phone to your ear or, in an effort to avoid neck strain, wearing a hands-free headset. Your client is giving you information in a quick, urgent tone. Your eyes are glued to the screen, searching various files for the ones you need, and your headset is beginning to hurt your ear.

Too much input! Too much stimulation! The richness and stillness of that time long ago is barely available to you now, except for the rare moments you might spend in a workshop or yoga class. These days when you walk, you are with a friend talking or have headphones in your ears moving you forward with music or an audio book. While you might have some awareness of the environment around you, you're more focused on getting in the requisite miles than taking time to stand in front of a tree and engage silently with its strong, solid presence.

What for your infant self was an effortless connection to natural rhythms is now lost in a cacophony of outer noise and chaos that fosters inner confusion. And that confusion keeps you from knowing how to reliably recapture the sense of wonder and ease that had once been your natural habitat.

No matter how much we learn and know, ultimately life is a mystery, an intricately wrapped package whose colorful ribbons are difficult to tease apart and smooth out. And what most of us want more than anything is a simple way to unknot the ties that bind us. As a lifelong seeker and a healer, the most elusive understanding is why it's so hard to consistently do the things I know help me feel like my best self. Sometimes it's all flowing, sometimes I'm stuck in my own muck; but after years of playing "good girl, bad girl," I've gathered tools and inner resources that help me, as Nike so succinctly puts it, *Just do it* (or, as one neuroscientist riffed, "just do it, a little bit more than you don't").

It's so easy to get caught up in learning some new complex system, or pick up countless books and DVD's to help guide you, and then find yourself on to the next new thing, leaving what you had previously gathered to collect dust. It still is my default mode when I'm tired and stressed, grabbing at things and thinking, "maybe this will do it, maybe that will be the answer, maybe that new shirt in the perfect shade of blue will make me feel better."

Yet in all of that reaching outward and searching for salvation, a single theme has always run through my mind: "The basics are the basics for a reason; because if you actually take time to do them, they work!" Basics like:

- Breathing fully and consciously.

- Drinking plenty of water.

- Eating more fruits and vegetables, fewer processed foods and sweets.

- Moving your body every day.

- Making time for quiet, contemplation and stillness.

Variations on these topics are in every issue of every health and beauty magazine. The headlines try to make it sound like something new and exciting, but how often do we need to be told that exercise and broccoli are good for us? Apparently often because most of us still haven't quite gotten the message. If they are so universal and so good for us, the question remains, "Why don't I do the things I know make me feel my best? How can I live in a way that keeps me connected to my heart and the deep wisdom and mercy that reside there?"

Running and Returning

There was a great sense of relief when I learned the concept of *running and returning*. The ancient Kabbalists teach that, "*If your heart runs {from its ultimate connection}, return it to the Place* (Makom)." Makom is a name of God, meaning the Omnipresent; it reminds us that everything in existence is imbued with Divinity, and also points directly to the idea that we are always moving toward and away from our wholeness.

In my late 20's I wrote a journal entry that foreshadowed this teaching:

> I forget to remember that I know what I know, so I am going to write until it all becomes clear. The knowing began the moment I was conceived, a moment of love and heat and dampness in which I rooted myself and began to grow. And it ended the moment I was brought into a world that forced air into my lungs and light into my eyes and sound into my ears…the forgetting began and continued to grow until I realized that I would never be comfortable living in my own skin until I could figure out what was missing. What was missing was a clear connection to the Source of all life. No, not missing, hidden; not completely forgotten and yet not fully recognized.

We forget and remember, forget and remember. Years later I heard a Jewish fable that perfectly echoed what I'd written:

> When babies are born, they have full knowledge of God and the deeper mysteries. But at the moment of birth an angel comes and puts a finger just above the lip, whispering "Shhhhhh, forget everything, speak not of what you know." This creates the little hollow between the nose and upper lip, and is why we spend our lives searching for something that is right under our nose all along.

Longing is built into the very fiber of your being. It is a chord that is struck the day you are born and keeps reverberating, causing you to search for a spiritual path that brings harmony to your soul. We all long to connect with what we are completely immersed in, like the proverbial fish that doesn't know what water is because water is the very atmosphere of its existence.

This teaching helps us understand that cycling in and out is an essential part of being human, as we are reminded in these words from Ecclesiastes made famous in song by Pete Seeger — "A time to build up, a time to break down, A time to dance, a time to mourn, A time to cast away stones, a time to gather stones together."

The Forgetting Factor

When you recognize and accept the paradox that forgetting to do the things that support spiritual alignment is actually a part of life's continuum, you can begin to have some compassion for yourself and your own dance of starting and stopping. If fallow periods are a necessary part of planting and harvesting crops, then why would they not be part of a meditation practice, a yoga practice, or a healthy eating practice?

Remembering that truth can help shift the energy from stuck to fluid, bringing a sense of mercy and compassion to what seem like individual shortcomings and weaknesses. That in itself may be the very springboard that will get you off of the couch and onto the yoga mat, or out to the store for some fresh salad fixings instead of unearthing that frozen dinner hidden away as insurance.

Life is endlessly pulsating, shifting from expansion to stasis and every level in between. Even when things feel stuck and stagnant, there is an underlying quality of movement that is always available for us to tune into. Go underneath the stories of why you feel stuck and how that somehow makes you a 'bad person' as opposed to simply human. Remember to connect with this pulsating quality and see how it supports you in making a shift.

It's so easy when you're feeling low or stuck to think you'll always feel that way. The good times might not ever last nor were they meant to; but you can slowly increase their power by catching yourself in a downturn and taking even the smallest steps toward connecting with a vision of your larger self. It means never forgetting that without dark you cannot truly know light, and without sadness, happiness would cease to permeate in quite the same way with its precious sense of expansiveness.

Working off of the earlier idea of The Basics, I thought about the simple practices I've come back to over and over again when the world threatens to come crashing in, and came up with six key concepts that help set the stage for greater peace of mind. How? By developing an ability to be profoundly attuned and unconditionally kind to your self. By approaching the work of taking care of yourself from the inside out rather than the outside in. With that in place, you may just find it's easier to make choices that nurture your body; that you are responding with greater equanimity when the people in your life are driving you crazy; and that you can be in the world, with all of its chaos and pain, with an open and compassionate heart.

As you explore and play with these exercises and concepts, pay attention to your experience of the pulsating quality of running and returning. Keep in mind your natural tendency to forget how truly connected you are, within your holy body and beyond—remember that you are a conscious co-creator with the Infinite. Let this knowledge lead you back as you would a small child about to take the wrong path to the playground.

In that playground you are building a bridge, one that will take you from intellectual knowing to full presence knowing, from ideology to the ability to harvest from your own wisdom. The path to a peaceful heart is paved with kindness, a light touch, small steps and skillful use of these simple practices.

The Basics For Cultivating Joy and Resilience

⦿

Breathe
to connect to your inner knowing

Acclimate
to your own rhythms

Simplify
your thinking through inquiry

Initiate
small physical movements daily

Consult
your inner guidance system

Sanctify
daily life with gratitude

CHAPTER TWO

Breathe to Connect to Your Inner Knowing

All breath is movement. All movement originates with inhaling and exhaling. All movement becomes elaborated by the breadth of breath. Breath is an invitation for a greater intelligence to come and dance.

Emilie Conrad, *Life On Land*

ॐ

Your breath is the perfect vehicle for uniting more closely with yourself and your Source. You know how easy it is to get behind the wheel of your car, turn the key, back out of the driveway and find yourself at work half an hour later with little conscious recall of how you actually got there? If it's easy to lose track of yourself while maneuvering a complex piece of machinery, you can see how easy it is to never really think about breathing, which happens whether you're thinking about it or not.

But given that breath is the vehicle that drives us through life—far more critical even than food or liquid—how much farther might we get down life's highway with some care and focused attention given to it?

We walk through much of life in various split states; the head from the body, the torso from the legs, the dominant side from the non-dominant side. And we go through much of our day with our consciousness separate from the breath and with the breath separate from the full torso, and especially from the extremities. Automatic breathing keeps us alive but is far from the fullest expression of our life force. Like the car trip you can barely remember, disconnection from your breath leads to missing out on feeling fully connected to yourself.

How do you know when you've been disconnected from your breath or other parts of your being? It hits you in those moments when you suddenly come home to yourself, when you wake from the dream of running through life and really savor a perfectly buttered bite of toast or a streak of sun coming out from behind a cloud. In those moments you spontaneously take a deep breath and move from feeling like a walking head to remembering you are an embodied spirit.

Three Part Breath

This is the simplest thing you can do to center yourself, but remember simple doesn't always mean easy! In fact one of the reasons we tend to overlook the simplest, dare I say most <u>basic</u> things, is because life is complex and so we tend to look for equally complex solutions. And yet, simple is what helps us focus our awareness and tune our senses to clarity rather than confusion. It is like the sword of a Zen master cutting through delusion with swift and electrifying precision.

Taking a few moments to just be with your breathing is actually a radical act. It entails that you stop doing and simply be present in your body in this moment.

It also requires you to pay attention, and that might bring to the surface some uncomfortable feelings that you are usually busy trying to not experience fully. In those precious moments of quiet, you might also feel anxiety, fear, loneliness, craving or any number of less desirable emotions that are a natural part of being human.

We are afraid that if we let ourselves feel these difficult emotions we will be swept away by them when the opposite is true—by letting ourselves feel things fully with compassion and courage, they can move through us like wind through a chime, leaving only a resonant note behind.

 TRY THIS when you feel like you're in a hamster wheel or find yourself emotionally overreacting to outside stimuli.

- Sit or stand in a relaxed yet upright position. You want to feel supported by either the chair or the floor, spine erect but not stiff. Begin by emptying your lungs completely of breath, pulling your belly in and exhaling as fully as possible.

- As you begin to inhale, bring the breath down into your belly first, allowing the abdomen to expand. Your diaphragm is shaped like a parachute along the lower rim of the ribcage, moving down as it engages on the inhale and up as it releases on the exhale. Letting your belly relax gives your diaphragm space to engage fully and lower, making room for your lungs to expand more fully than in unconscious respiration.

- Now allow the breath to fill your chest from the bottom to the top, so that the last stage of the inhale expands into your upper chest and ribcage.

- When you are ready, exhale in the opposite direction, so that you release the breath from the top of the chest first and then through the lower chest, with the abdomen emptying and pulling in last.

Try placing one hand on the belly and the other on the upper chest to help you tangibly experience the flow of breath in and out of your body. The movements of this breath often feel counterintuitive, especially if you are primarily a chest or belly breather. By using three part breathing, you are expanding all the parts of your torso—pay attention to how it feels not just in the front of your body, but also the sides and back. Feel how many dimensions there are when you breathe this way.

If it feels at all uncomfortable or frustrating, take it slowly. Be patient, gentle and compassionate with your body as it tries on this new way of breathing. Most of the time we are barely using one fourth of our lungs' full capacity! With practice your secondary muscles of respiration, seldom utilized during normal shallow breathing, will come into play and allow you to take in more and more oxygen over time. This alone will give your nervous system more resilience, fluidity and calm.

Deepening Presence with Mantra

Once you are comfortable with the basic breath, begin to anchor your presence by adding a verbal touchstone or mantra. One of the most simple and beautiful declarations I know of is to simply announce "Here I am," and an evocative way to do it is with the Hebrew word *hineni* (hee-nay-nee). By declaring *hineni* we are offering our full spiritual presence, stating that we are ready and willing to show up for ourselves and for our relationship with the Divine.

Since biblical times, when both Abraham and Moses responded to the call of the Lord in this way, the word *hineni* offers a powerful statement of presence, purpose and possibility. It is so much more than simply saying "Yoo hoo, here I am, over here!" It is a way of saying to your heart, your soul and your Creator, "Here I am, ready and willing to be fully present, to offer myself up as part of the healing of the world through deepening my consciousness and my ability to serve with love."

Try saying *hineni* or *here I am* slowly and quietly as you breathe through your entire torso, using the basic three-part breath. Practice saying it any time you wake from an unconscious place and want to offer your intention to spend more time being aware of life's unfolding moments.

Another phrase that I find helpful, especially when I am struggling and life feels particularly challenging, is *ki tov* (kee tove) — *It is good.* This is what God declared after each phase of creation. Breathing into your heart and declaring *ki tov* about whatever is happening can help you recall that life's difficulties are also opportunities. They help to polish your rough edges and learn where your true strength lies.

ℵ **What favorite mantras or verbal touchstones bring you a sense of spiritual support and connection?**

CHAPTER THREE

Acclimate to Your Own Rhythms

For the rhythm of life is a powerful beat.
Puts a tingle in your fingers and a tingle in your feet.
Rhythm on the inside, rhythm on the street
The rhythm of life is a powerful beat.

Cy Coleman and Dorothy Fields, *Sweet Charity*

त्ऱ

It's hard to feel your own rhythms when the noise of the world is always pressing in on you. Once upon a time, your entire experience was rocked in a cradle of warmth and movement. That was all you knew, and it reverberates in you still; but now it takes effort to plug into these deeper rhythms.

We are born into a world of vibration, floating in a fluid sack moved by the drum of our mother's heart. Our first sense of ourselves is one of being vibrated in a human body, pulsing to primordial rhythms and currents.

That doesn't change as we move into life outside of our mother's body, but it is part of what gets lost — part of the forgetting. Everything in life has its own vibration, and the energy moving within and around us has its own vibration.

We spend most of our waking hours looking out and taking in, pulling words and images in through our eyes and ears. It's like being a submarine with its periscope permanently up and out, scanning the surface for input or to defend against would-be attackers. It can be stimulating and exciting and educational. It can also dull us to the quieter signals of our soul, and confuse the mind so that the heart's clear knowing can't be heard.

How do you know when you are in tune with yourself? Do you get there by walking in a park or wooded area, by dancing alone with the stereo blasting, by working with the tender green plants in your garden?

First stop: When the rhythms of the world have you feeling like you're on a merry-go-round, the best place to start is to just STOP. Stop talking, stop listening to the radio or watching TV, stop bopping around on the Internet, stop picking up the phone or checking e-mail.

Walk away from the desk or turn off the TV. Take one mindful breath, then another. Don't force it, simply let your breath come into your awareness and really feel it moving through your body.

Then look: From wherever you are, sitting, standing or walking, begin looking with a soft yet attentive gaze at whatever is around you. Really take in the contours of your coffee mug, the crumbs on the table, the leaves outside your window, the sacred objects placed on your altar long ago.

Now listen: After spending some time communing with the visual world, close your eyes and begin to connect with the sounds around you. The dishwasher might be whirring into a new cycle, the clock may be ticking, the chirp of birds and whoosh of passing cars may be coming in through your window. Don't reach out to grasp at any sounds, simply let them come into your awareness one at a time, then with the fullness of layers of proximity and distance.

If you have done this—truly stopping and paying exquisite attention to everything you see, feel and hear—you have stepped into mindful awareness, the hallmark of meditation. It doesn't necessarily have to happen sitting cross-legged on the floor, although that level of consistent practice will pave the way for bringing mindfulness to more of your life. But simply taking time to listen, look and feel your moment-to-moment experience, without judging or changing it, is a practice you can call forth at any time.

Remember this optical illusion? When you first look, you usually see only one image, either a chalice or two faces coming in for a kiss. But once the other image is pointed out to you, you cannot NOT see it!

It's a bit like what happens when we overly focus on some things—usually negative—while missing the obvious beauty of everything else around us. We see only part of what is true and miss out on the experience that comes from relating fully to all of the gradations of color and form that exist in our immediate environment. Try shifting your focus from foreground to background more consistently—take in the forest while acknowledging each tree.

Attune To Your Inner Rhythms

Inner rhythms can be subtle and subconscious, or loud and determined. Something in you might be screaming out for some time in a park or by the water, especially when you realize that your feet have only touched concrete, carpet and car pedals for days on end.

Movement in any direction will ultimately lead to movement in a specific direction. Remember Newton's law? A body in motion tends to stay in motion. And undirected movement will sometimes lead you to places you didn't know you needed to go.

 TRY THIS when you realize that you haven't felt like yourself for a while; when you are feeling over-stimulated and moving through life on autopilot.

Put on your favorite music as loud as is comfortable. Stand still for a few moments and allow the rhythm and melody to seep in before beginning to move spontaneously. Swirling, swaying, jumping, arms waving or still—allow the music to take your body where it longs to go, with no thought to how it looks, just how it *feels*.

- Play with varying your movement to focus on just your hips or your shoulders.

- Articulate each joint—elbows, wrists, ankles, toes, fingers and knees. Flex, rotate, stretch and send conscious focus to places you normally don't experience fully.

- Become outwardly still at different points in the dance and experience how the music moves inside of you.

- Allow yourself to move slowly when the music is fast, and fast when the music is slow. Really let the movement arise from your most authentic sense of what your body needs in the moment, no matter what the music is prompting you to do.

When you feel ready to come to complete stillness, take time to stay with that before moving on to something else. You may want to lie on the floor and let your body be fully supported as it experiences the energy that is now surging through your cells.

Take a moment to write about your experience and the thoughts and feelings that it evoked. This is a great practice to bring relief and reconnection after a period of intense mental stimulation, emotional exhaustion or physical disconnection through too much sitting or unconscious, repetitive movement. Come back to it again and again, giving yourself new opportunities to experience yourself as a fully embodied being, one who is comfortable owning every expression of energy—vivid, languid, ecstatic, enchanted, melancholy, introspective and all of the nuances in between.

 TRY THIS when your focus has been too external; when you've lost sight of your basic goodness and an awareness of how much you've actually accomplished in life.

I am good at dreams, I am good at dreams
Bad at savings bonds, fashion magazines
I am good at dreams, I am good at dreams.
I am good at wind, I am good at stone,
I am good at rain and good at all alone
I am good at you and good at home.
John Gorka, *Good*

How often do you allow yourself to acknowledge all of the things you are good at? I mean *all* of the things, not just obvious ones like being good at your job or good at baking cakes (which I'm sure makes you very popular with the lucky recipients!).

One day when I was feeling really blue, I followed a suggestion I'd heard from a spiritual teacher: make a list of fifty things you are good at or proud of having accomplished. Not ten, not twenty or twenty-five, but FIFTY. So I began, and for the first half of the list I was on a good roll—the career I've built as a bodywork therapist, the articles I've had published, some big moves I've made to different geographic locations, stuff that is easy to acknowledge and pinpoint.

Then I had to really stretch, and in the stretching some intriguing things came out:

#31 – I pick up dance steps quickly and easily.

#36 – I possess an uncanny memory for phone numbers because of their inherent rhythm.

#41 – My love of trees and sense of them as friends and allies is real and important.

#47 – The gift of being present to offer healing and prayers with Ellen as her father left his body.

Try this for yourself. Take at least 20 minutes and do it all in one sitting, rather than starting and coming back to it later when you've run out of obvious ideas, or dragging it out because you're having trouble thinking of things. Push to unearth what lies beneath your most stellar qualities and accomplishments. Let yourself really sink into the goodness that you inherently are and the unique ways in which your natural talents, abilities and yes, even quirks, reveal themselves.

What did you learn about yourself by doing this exercise? What do you know about yourself in a different way that you might not have been aware of before you started the list? What did you remember that gave you a new awareness of your essential self and all of the ways that it weaves through even seemingly mundane activities?

CHAPTER FOUR

Simplify Your Thinking Through Inquiry

*We are entering the dimension where
we have control – the inside.*

Byron Katie, *Loving What Is*

❧

Thinking—have you ever really considered how much space thinking takes up in your day? And, more importantly, have you determined the difference between critical thinking that helps you understand things in the world around you, or resolve a problem, or decide how best to approach a difficult matter, and the unending whir of judgments, repetitive worries, and hamster wheel neuroses that seem to float about your brain unbidden?

Without some specific tools for reigning in an unruly mind, it's kind of like trying to herd cats (ever tried herding even one cat?). Thoughts float around in our heads like a hive of angry bees, and trying to swat them away leaves us stung and tender. We keep going around and around in circles of *"What if?"* and *"I can't believe he said"* and *"Why didn't I?"*—thoughts that are nearly impossible to step away from and don't really bring us to any satisfying sense of resolution.

The Buddha taught a simple yet profound truth about thoughts and created a whole system of living to help us grasp and make use of this insight: Thoughts arise and it is our attachment to them that brings about suffering. Think about that.

We love to assume that our thoughts are our own, independent and unique products of our personality and experience. But if we take some time to really look at our thoughts with some detachment, as if they were happening outside of us, something else starts to emerge.

We can begin to see that thoughts are repetitive, that they cycle around and around, and that we often keep a commentary going about everything that happens, good, bad and indifferent. They run roughshod over us and keep us from being happy, from feeling compassion for ourselves or others, or simply from getting a good night's sleep.

Inquire Within

There are many different methods for looking at our thoughts and working with them consciously. One of the most direct and helpful methods I've discovered is simply called The Work, developed by a woman named Byron Katie. A friend introduced me to it at a time in my life when my head was swimming with so many negative thoughts it felt like I was drowning. It's a systematic method of inquiry that helps stop painful thoughts in their tracks and brings us back to the truth of the present moment, the only place where we can ever be fully free.

Katie states that there are only three kinds of business in this world—my business, your business and God's business—and if our thoughts are focused on anyone's business but our own, pain will surely follow because we aren't in control of their business.

What does this really mean? Take a moment to reflect on a recent bout of mental distress. What was your point of focus? If you were worrying about how your husband doesn't exercise enough or drinks too much beer after work, then you were in his business. If you were getting bent out of shape because it rained for three days straight, then you were in God's business. You may have felt affected by these things, but they were not truly within your power to change.

Sometimes, just realizing that you are in someone else's business when you start to feel anxious and upset can help shift your perspective and invite more peace of mind. In a world that is so out of control, we may not even see how much we are trying to control things with our thoughts of how they should be.

How exhausting! We think that our partner should change, or the woman driving slowly in the Mercedes should move out of the left lane, or it should just stop raining already, damn it! And yet our partner stays on the couch and the lady in the Mercedes stays in the left lane and the grey skies keep raining on our parade.

When you stop and ask yourself *Whose business am I in right now?* you take a step back and shift your awareness from outside to inside. You begin to take control of the only thing that you really do have control over — your own response to the truth of what is happening in any given moment. You gain a little more space and a little more peace when you let anyone's business but your own be exactly what it is.

This may sound like complacency, but it actually gives you a chance to respond more peacefully and purposefully. If your husband doesn't get up off the couch, you can take a walk on your own and feel how happy it makes your body to be moving. If Mercedes lady sticks to the left lane, you can move right rather than tailgate and perhaps rear-end her if she brakes unexpectedly. If the rain keeps coming down, you can clean out the closet you've been meaning to get to or rent the movie you've wanted to see since last summer.

 TRY THIS when your brain feels like it's on a hamster wheel, when you are stuck in blame and anger, or when you are confused about how to deal with a person who is driving you crazy.

The core of The Work is four questions that you ask yourself when you are experiencing a painful thought, such as *My husband should get off the couch.* The fact that he *is* on the couch means that you are fighting reality, and fighting reality only brings pain and suffering (like any thoughts you become attached to). So with this painful thought, or any other, ask yourself:

Is it true? (that he should not be on the couch?) If you really look at the reality of it and still think yes, then ask the following.

Can you absolutely know that it's true? *Hmmm, well that's what I think but it is what's happening, so no, I can't absolutely know that it's true that he shouldn't be if he is!*

The next two questions are where things really become interesting:

How do you react when you believe that thought? *Well, I get so mad I can't really look at him. I leave the room and sit and stew in my office. I bang the pots and pans around in the kitchen so he'll know I'm really pissed.* (Not very fun or fulfilling, huh?)

Who would you be without the thought? *I'd be a woman whose husband likes to watch TV more than she does. I would be more peaceful and at ease. I would focus more on what I want to do than on what he's doing or not doing.*

Some of the biggest "Ah-ha's" occur when you complete the inquiry with what Katie calls *turnarounds,* which are a way of experiencing the opposite of what you believe. Find ways to turn your judgment around towards yourself or an apparent opposite and then find at least three specific, genuine examples of how each turnaround is true in your life. Here is how turnarounds can be applied to the situation above:

41

My husband should not get off the couch. (Examples: 1. That's where he wants to be, for now. 2. That's his way of relaxing. How can I really know what's best for him? 3. That leaves me free to do something I really want to do, without thinking of pleasing him.)

I should get off the couch. (1. Of course I should! I want to do something else, not watch TV. 2. It's not honest for me to stay on the couch when I don't want to be there. 3. If I stay on the couch when I don't really want to, I'll get upset.)

I should get off my husband. (1. I should stop judging my husband for not getting off the couch because it makes me miserable. 2. It annoys him and results in separation between us. It's kinder, both to him and to myself, to get off his case. 3. If I stay in my own business, rather than try to improve him, I'm always happier.)

When you really take time to question the thoughts and judgments that cause you the most pain, you begin to see how it truly is the thoughts themselves that are the problems. Releasing the attachment to painful thoughts opens up a vast range of possible responses and actions. When you stop telling your husband to get off the couch and just go out and do what makes you happy, he might be more likely to get up and join you. And if not, you'll feel more fulfilled and satisfied with yourself, which is the only true path to a peaceful heart.

CHAPTER FIVE

Initiate Small Physical Movements Daily

If your spine is flexible,
you're young no matter your age:
If your spine is not flexible,
you're old no matter your age.
It's as simple as that.

Gay Hendricks, PhD. *Achieving Vibrance*

❧

In my mind each morning as I slowly return to consciousness, I see myself heading directly to my yoga mat to perform a lovely series of wake-up stretches and postures to begin my day. In reality, by the time I'm actually out of bed, it most often looks more like this: put the kettle on, feed the cat, have that first cup of kukicha tea and some fruit to get my system going, read something inspirational, use the bathroom, spend some time in meditation and, oh yes, do a little stretching before I take my seat on the cushion.

The best-laid plans often do go astray, and there is always so much that needs to be done it's easy to avoid getting our bodies in motion. We become thinking, talking heads, disconnected from the physical forms that carry us through life, paying little attention to our bodies unless something hurts or stops working as expected. And yet motion — fluid, multi-directional motion — is exactly what our muscles and nervous system were designed for.

Most of our daily life is spent in linear, forward movement, although sometimes it certainly feels we are moving backward! We sit in cars, moving forward down roads, arms held up, eyes trained on the space that keeps opening up in front of us. We surge through our days, lifting laptops, holding phones to ears, placing objects in front of us, tapping away at keyboards or reaching for laundry to be folded and placed in drawers, which move linearly on their tracks too.

When do we have a chance to be fluid? When do we even remember that we *are* fluid, that even the bones that hold us up, keeping our muscles in place and organs held safe, are alive, juicy, marrow-filled tissue? When we don't spend time in water, or take time to move fluidly and intuitively rather than purposefully, our natural lubrication dries up. Our tissues become dense and compact, losing elasticity and their natural tendency to be pliant and flowing.

Move Your Spine In Every Direction

It's easy to forget that our bodies were engineered for movement. Every bone and muscle has a function, and ever since we have stood on two legs, we've run, walked, crouched, squatted, kneeled and yes, sometimes even sat.

But now we mostly sit, and sit, and sit some more until our spine is compressed and our hamstring muscles at the back of the thighs are wound tighter than a ball of string. You find yourself getting up and feeling like the Tin Man from the Wizard of Oz crying "Oil can, oil can!"

One of the keys to pliability is motion, plain and simple. It doesn't necessarily take a lot, but it does take consistency and conscientiousness. Our tissues warm and moisten and release when we allow them to do what they were created to do. And a great way to start is with your spine, the very core of your physical being.

 TRY THIS when your back aches from sitting too long at the computer or in the car; a little bit every day to keep your energy flowing and your joints limber and lubricated.

Begin with some standing warm ups. Letting your arms hang very loosely from your shoulders, gently turn your body from side to side. Your arms will come along for the ride and become part of the momentum as you move more quickly and make the motion bigger. You might even let the arm coming across the front of your body lift and land on the opposite shoulder or upper arm, bringing your hand into a loose fist to offer a bit of massage to the other side.

When you feel ready, let your body come to stillness. Take a moment to simply breathe and feel the energy from just this small amount of movement.

Now it's time to work from the bottom of the spine to the top:

- Begin in an upright, seated position, with your back away from the back of the chair so there is room to move. Gently, slowly arch the small of your back, taking a full, easy in-breath. Then flatten the small of your back, breathing out as you move.

- Let the movements begin in a subtle way, first just in your pelvis, then bringing more of your spine into the curving forward and arching back. Now move even more deeply into flexing forward and extending back, becoming aware of the natural movement of your head and upper back that follows as you continue. Your whole spine and torso will come into play as you warm to the movement.

- Don't strain or push. Allow yourself to work as slowly as feels comfortable, and focus on all of the sensations that arise in your body as you move through each part of the exercise.

- When you feel warmed up and have gone as far into the stretch as possible while seated, bring yourself into a standing position. Let your feet be about hip width apart, knees soft.

• Continue with these movements, again starting with just a rocking of the pelvis, and then making them bigger and using more of your body. Gradually include opening and closing the arms as you extend back and then flex forward; remember to focus on your breath, inhaling as you open back and exhaling as you fold forward.

• Feel as if you are opening and releasing any pent up anger, frustration or sadness as you open your arms and chest; feel as if you are bringing in fresh energy, nurturance and calm as you fold your arms in and bend forward.

• End by standing still, knees soft and body aligned as if you were being held by a piece of string at the top of your head. Feel the new energy moving through your spine, pelvis, arms and legs. Enjoy all of the sensations that this movement has provided.

CHAPTER SIX

Consult Your Inner Guidance System

But like a compass seeking north
There lives in me a still sure spirit part
Clouds of doubt are cut asunder
By the lightning and the thunder
Shining from the compass of my heart.

David Crosby, *Compass*

৵৶

We are receiving information all of the time. It's coming from outside sources like books, magazines, the Internet and television. It's also coming from inside with promptings to trust or not trust certain people, to turn right instead of left when you are lost and find your way to an intersection. But those inner messages can feel fleeting and ephemeral, making them seem less reliable than an Internet search or a trusted advisor.

Much of the time these outside sources, or simply our own lack of attention, can block the subtler messages that offer great value and assistance in living our daily lives. You may have a GPS in your car, but how do you consistently access the inner Global Positioning System that helps you navigate through relationship issues, work stress, and a desire to feel connected to something beyond your individual life?

When we want a friend to feel welcome in our home, we take specific steps—vacuum the floors, wash and put away the dishes that have piled up, maybe bake some homemade treat to serve with tea. We create a space that is inviting and conducive to inspired conversation and an atmosphere of ease.

In order to really hear the subtle messages we are always receiving, it helps to develop rituals that allow us to attune to and welcome them in. Just as a radio can be set to a station that pulls in classical music, you can fine-tune your inner listening to receive guidance from your deepest knowing.

Oracles are ritual divination tools that help you to access wisdom from higher realms. They use beautiful images and evocative words to help you learn about yourself and understand what you need to know regarding a particular issue or yearning. They can range from the ancient wisdom of the I Ching and Tarot to the newer sets of Angel cards and Goddess decks.

I keep a bowl of Angel cards on my altar and often pull a few when I sit to meditate. I love them for their simplicity and whimsy—they are small cards with a single word on each, such as Compassion, Trust, Balance, Synthesis, with an accompanying image of an angel embodying the energy of that word. Sometimes I pull just one, but more often I pull a few to see what the connections might be.

When I was beginning to write this book, I pulled a set of 2 or 3 cards over the course of several days, not even focusing on a specific question or issue but simply to give me some guidance and insight for my meditation. Each day, whatever cards I pulled included the Communication card. One day it was Joy/Communication, then it was Truth/Communication, and the next day it was Freedom/Communication/Faith.

After years of wrestling with what to write, how strong my commitment to writing really was, often thinking it didn't matter if anything ever got written by me, here I was feeling ready and here was my hand being guided to this same card on three successive days. And, since I am the one responsible for making meaning of my life, this felt like a clear answer to a question I didn't even know I was asking. Ready or not, it was time to finally write a book that had been gestating in me for a long time.

 TRY THIS when you feel confused and long for some guidance; when you are ready to receive guidance from your subconscious or want some inspiration for the day or for a specific project.

If you own a deck of cards that you bought long ago but tucked away on a shelf, get them out and keep them where you will be more likely to use them. If you don't own any oracle systems, find time to visit your local bookstore or metaphysical store and explore what is out there.

What appeals to you most is what will work best; there is an incredible array of artistry and imagery available. The decks themselves don't have the answers; they are simply vehicles for your own intuitive wisdom to reveal itself. So find a deck (or two or three, if you choose) and begin to work with them to develop your inner GPS.

Set a space for your intuitive play as you would for that friend you've invited for tea. You may want to:

- Choose a special scarf or cloth for storing and laying out your deck.

- Light a candle to warm and illuminate the space.

- Take a few moments to center yourself with three slow, deep breaths; trust that you will receive the best guidance for your question or quandary.

- Have your favorite journal and pen(s) handy for capturing insights and ideas.

- Make a cup of tea, anoint yourself with some pure essential oils, play some music that inspires you; allow yourself to feel sensually nourished and cared for.

Once you have set the space, meditate on a question you have been wrestling with or an issue that needs clarity. Rather than ask for a simple yes or no answer, which may or may not actually be helpful, simply ask "What do I need to know about _____?" or "What is this situation helping me to understand?" or even "Please offer me guidance and encouragement for this day."

Before going on to read what the accompanying text has to offer, take some time to sit quietly with the image and/or words you have received. Allow your inner knowing to rise and meet it with whatever feelings, impressions, sensations, words or snippets of song that might spontaneously come forth.

Some oracle systems I love for their simplicity and ease of use:

Angel Cards *The Original Angel Cards: Inspirational Messages and Meditations* by Kathy Tyler and Joy Drake, small cards with a single evocative word and playful image for contemplation.

Runes Norse symbols on small white stones accompanied by a beautifully written text, *The Book of Runes* by Ralph Blum.

I've also used ones that can be more involved, such as:

Tarot decks The very first Tarot reader I worked with used the round, feminist oriented *Motherpeace* deck, with accompanying book by Vicki Noble, and that was the first oracle deck I ever bought. I have also loved using the brilliant hues and mystical teachings of the *Osho Zen* deck.

The Kabbalah Deck Scholar Edward Hoffman's beautiful deck and book illuminate the meaning of the letters of the

Hebrew alphabet and the 10 distinct energies called *sephirot* in the Kabbalistic Tree of Life.

I Ching Requires three coins that you toss to come up with a pattern, and the ancient, venerable Chinese *Book of Changes* to explain what those patterns mean. Like tarot decks there are many variations on the I Ching. Find one whose language and imagery appeal to you; some versions are older and the wording can be somewhat cryptic and difficult to understand.

Cultivate Guidance Through Artistic Expression

"Me?" you ask. "I'm not an artist!" But you are, in the way that every one of us holds beauty and creativity and a desire to express our deepest selves in meaningful ways.

When was the last time you allowed yourself space and time and emotional safety to let your visions out in a tangible way? Do the long ago voices of parents or teachers deter you from expressing yourself through painting, writing, or music?

In Africa, music and work go hand in hand. I saw a beautiful documentary called *Throw Down Your Heart,* about the journey of brilliant, eclectic banjo player Béla Fleck through four African nations in search of the origins of his instrument. One woman he met was a leader of song in her community. She would sing a line and in call and response style the other women would sing it back, all of them working on the day's food preparation or dishwashing. The tasks were repetitive and tiresome, but the joy of song carried them through and deepened their sense of community.

There is a saying, "if you can walk you can dance, if you can speak you can sing." Creative expression is part of our collective DNA — it begs us to draw outside the lines and make a joyful noise unto the Lord when our spirit is moved.

When we shake things up through art, music, dance or any other form of expression that *takes us outside of mental constructs*, we open ourselves to the mystery of creation itself. We create the chance to learn something new about ourselves, to connect to something hidden in our essential self that cannot be thought into presence. We take a step towards knowing things that will help us to be the person we inherently are but don't always have access to.

Years ago in an undergraduate art class, I didn't feel confident drawing or painting but discovered that I loved making collages. Choosing the images and words, then juxtaposing them to convey my inner impulses, was simple yet powerful. I often make collage cards for friends, holding that person in my heart as I pick components that reflect who they are to me or what I know they are thinking about and working on in their lives at that time. It's amazing to play with the elements and see how the use of images, words and space always reflects the moment at hand.

 TRY THIS when you want to form a visual expression of an important inner call or urge, like meeting your life partner, deepening your spiritual practice or cultivating more beauty and self-care into your life, or when you need to move beyond the language of words and into the language of imagery and magic.

Collage is an art form that anyone can do. All it takes is a pile of magazines and catalogs, scissors, a piece of poster board and some glue. Begin by contemplating a problem or area where you have felt blocked or stifled, or something that you want to receive intuitive guidance about. You can do this in silence, or play some evocative music to help stimulate introspection and creativity.

Go through your collection of magazines and cut out any images and words that appeal to you or seem to speak to this issue. Don't worry about whether or not something is "right" or "best." Just keep cutting until you feel satisfied that you have more than enough to work with.

Take a few moments to sit with your eyes closed. Relax into your breathing and allow yourself to simply be as you are in the moment, with your questions, concerns, excitement, uncertainty, or great vision of a future possibility. Give yourself this time to really open up to something you don't yet know much about.

Now sift through what you have cut out and begin placing words and images on the poster board. Some will naturally want to be next to each other. Some will want to overlap and others will need more space around them. Trust that whatever feels right is right, then trim each piece and glue it into place.

I like to cut some pieces with curved edges and some with straight edges, and that too affects the overall energy of the collage. You might want to grab some colored markers, stickers or glitter pens to add words, doodles, or squiggles of your own that bring a different energy and sense of connection to the piece.

Take some time when you are done to really take in what you have created and how it makes you feel. Are you excited? Sad? Angry? Uplifted? Inspired? You may want to spend a few moments journaling about the experience and any shift that has occurred around your original question or concern. Hang it where you will see it regularly to remind you of what you know and where you are headed.

Knowing

There are millions of ways to know
Listen, here comes one now.
Open your hand, let it rest
in the palm
and wait.
Don't try to chat with it
or ask it to lunch.

It will lie still as
a sleeping cat and
reveal all you need to know
as it begins to groom
upon awakening.

Or it may come dancing in on the
tempestuous toss of trees
before a thunderstorm.
Much can be learned in the
act of witnessing,

heart open, mind at rest,
ears attuned, twitching with
unfamiliar vibrations.

In the center of this whirlwind
or the center of your hand,
you catch the end of the thread
binding you to
the Mystery.

SHR ©2008

CHAPTER SEVEN

Sanctify Daily Life
With Gratitude

Let me learn to praise and bless,
let me learn to praise,
Let me learn to praise and bless,
for what I praise in others is You.

Jason Shulman

❧

M other Theresa is famous for having said, "We may not be able to do great things, but we can do small things with great love." This may be the wisest hidden-in-plain-sight spiritual truth of all — it is the quality of attention we bring to what we do that brings the juice of holiness to every action.

We hear a lot about gratitude these days, but have you really thought about what gratitude is and why it is so powerful?

On the most basic level it makes us feel better to think about and appreciate all that we have in our lives — a roof over one's head, enough food to eat, people who love us warts and all, a hot shower to help us start the day — than to focus on what we don't have, which often just leads to a pity party.

On its deepest level, gratitude is a way of taking our place in the circle of life. It shows that you acknowledge you are here for a reason, a unique and complex piece of All-That-Is. There is a prayer that is said by religiously observant Jews each morning the very moment they become aware of being conscious: *"Thank You for mercifully reawakening my soul within me, great is Your trust."*

WOW — Great is Your trust. The life force awakens us with tremendous trust and mercy to do something worthwhile with our allotted time here. We acknowledge being given a fresh chance each day to do more good than harm, to add something positive to the collective consciousness, to offer our time in service to something other than our individual self.

What a privilege…what an honor…what a mantra for giving shape and direction to a day that might otherwise start with thoughts of "oh shit, today I have to…" You may still have those thoughts — worry is as much a part of life as anything — but when you shine the light of awareness on gratitude for the opportunity to be part of a larger energy, the worry thoughts slip further out to the edges where the light is not so bright.

I remember something my first spiritual teacher, Hilda Charlton, used to say. When I met her in 1986, Hilda was an elderly woman, a vibrant, passionate lover of God and teacher of all things spiritual and metaphysical. People had started coming to learn from her many years before, when she returned quite changed after two decades of living and studying with different spiritual masters in India.

In the beginning she spoke to small groups gathered in someone's living room in New York City; over the years, as people brought friends who brought other friends, these gatherings expanded to several hundred people meeting in a sanctuary on the grounds of the Cathedral of St. John the Divine in upper Manhattan, which is when I began attending.

Hilda was somewhat eccentric and very spiritually evolved, but her teaching was in plain language and she usually referred to her students as "kids" (even when some of those kids were in their 50's and 60's). I remember her always encouraging us to remember God, serve God, and love God, and saying that one of the best ways to get spiritual direction was to wake up every day and say out loud "Good morning God! What are you up to today? I want to be a part of it! Thank you!"

The main message here is that *when we make a conscious effort to engage with the Source of Being, we will be more engaged with everything.* If we are each simply waves in the ocean of life, it is up to us to remember that we always have that vast realm pulsing within us, and are not simply the momentary event of a single swell—even when that swell feels like the biggest, gnarliest wave that the most intrepid surfer wouldn't attempt to ride.

TRY THIS when you're feeling blue and aren't sure what it's about—or perhaps you do know but feel totally stuck — and want a simple, reliable way to lift your spirits.

The 7-Day Grateful Heart Challenge

For one week, as soon as you realize you are awake each morning, give thanks for the fact that you have been given the gift of consciousness. Ask for the opportunity to serve in some way, great or small. Use one of the phrases above and take your first waking moments to say it to yourself or out loud if you have the privacy to do so. Clearly the first statement, "Thank You for mercifully reawakening my soul within me, great is Your trust" strikes a more somber and awe-filled note, while "Good morning God! What are you up to today? I want to be a part of it! Thank you!" brings a feeling of lightness and mirth.

Decide which tone would best serve you based on how you've been holding life lately; has it been feeling heavy or have you been playing it too loose? Try choosing one and sticking with it for the whole week, like a mantra or affirmation that will remind you of the fact that life is a precious gift that ought not be taken for granted. Sit with the phrase in your mind and heart before getting out of bed and starting your day. You may want to journal about what the phrase is evoking within you, how it is impacting your feelings and actions.

Sanctify Your Meals

When I was a Girl Scout, one of my favorite things about the experience was going on weekend camping trips. We'd sing songs on the bus ride out into the country, perform skits for one another at the Saturday night bonfire while eating s'mores, and enjoy the time gathering wood for our fires and clambering over boulders or wading in streams.

Before each meal, we'd also sing a song of praise to give thanks for our meal. There was Johnny Appleseed: "Oh the Lord is good to me, and so I thank the Lord, for giving me the things I need, the sun and the rain and the apple seed, the Lord is good to me." There was another lovely tune we sang that was simply a repetition of the words "Gracias Señor, Hallelujah." We took turns choosing which one to sing, connecting with each other and the food, enjoying a moment of gratitude and grace before digging in. Because we had gathered the wood, made the fire and prepared everything ourselves with only the simplest tools, we had much to be thankful for by the time we ate!

Whether it is a solemn bowing of the head and recitation of a proscribed prayer, a song, or a silly yet heartfelt "Rubba-dub-dub, thank the Lord for the grub, AMEN" try taking a moment before you eat to really connect with the food in front of you and everything about it. Give thanks for the farmers, the packers, the truckers, the grocery clerks, the animal that gave its life for your meal, the carrot and zucchini that were once alive in the dirt, the cook who added flavor and thoughtful preparation to each thing on your plate. In the rush of our lives, it is too easy to forget how much goes into the fact that we are able to eat as much as we want, and often exactly what we are in the mood for at any given meal. Taking a moment to acknowledge all that went into the food before you is a simple yet profound act of truth.

There is a reason that it is called "saying grace"—pausing, reflecting on the great fortune of having plenty of food to eat and plenty of choices, and connecting with each step in bringing that food to us in this exact moment, is truly an act of grace. We may take longer to chew, savoring and really tasting each bite, literally being graceful rather than mindlessly plowing through to get to whatever is scheduled next.

Take a Hint From Moses

One of the most amazing things about the Jewish faith in which I was raised is that there is a blessing for everything…and I mean EVERYTHING!

It starts with the blessing for coming back to life each morning. There are blessings for wine and for bread, for washing hands before a meal, for seeing a rainbow, and for the first fruit of the season. There is even a blessing of gratitude for having a bowel movement, praising the Creator of orifices for their ability to work correctly (now isn't that something to offer praise and thanks for—imagine if they didn't?!?). It reminds us that everything is indeed holy, from the loftiest vision to the earthiest bodily function.

I don't know all of those blessings the way rigorously observant Jews do, but my life is deliciously informed by the fact that they exist. The path of blessing is deep and wide, and we have only to step into its flow and sanctify as many moments of our lives as possible. With attention and gratitude, we remember that we are an integral part of All-That-Is and take responsibility for our impact on the whole.

CHAPTER EIGHT

The True Harvest

The true harvest of life is intangible.
It is as the tints of morning and evening.
It is a little stardust caught...
a segment of the rainbow.

Henry David Thoreau

༝༝

When I was in college, my parents sent me a birthday package that included a framed image with the above quote. These words have sustained me through times both difficult and rich with satisfaction.

Another quote I find helpful is from the Buddha's teachings and tells us to "Abandon any hope of fruition." In other words, don't do your spiritual practices because you expect a specific outcome (usually that your life will be better than it is right now). Each of these phrases help to remind us that what really matters is being as present to each moment as possible, to remain open to all of life as it presents itself, and to celebrate being just because you are here as life is endlessly unfolding. While you may hope for the best, true grace comes from greeting the circumstances of each day with as much clarity, humor and fluidity as possible.

The practices that have been presented here are like blazes on a wooded trail. They are markers that can help you make your journey with a sense of purpose, forward movement and ease, confident that someone has been here before you and knows the territory. You can only develop a peaceful heart through practice—kind of like getting to Carnegie Hall. Choose to spend a bit of time each day doing something that reminds you of your basic goodness, strength, resilience and joy. All of those live underneath or alongside the difficulties, fears and disturbances.

Even a master like Baryshnikov comes back to the barre each day to keep his form clean and lines strong; yet if he never stepped away from the barre we would not be dazzled by his particular expression of movement through space. Let the forms give you a container in which to learn and trust your unique dance.

This crazy world is a multihued puzzle filled with beauty, pain, wonder and awe. Focus on one point too closely and you lose the entire picture. Focus too widely and you can miss the subtle intricacies that make it all worthwhile—the scent of maple syrup as it hits your hot oatmeal; the softness of fur as you idly pet your cat at the end of a busy day; the smile of a stranger bopping his head to the music pouring in from his iPod as the subway lurches and sways. Learn to dance in the field between big picture and specific detail, and feel the beat of your peaceful heart.

And always, remember to

Make good effort... with great kindness.

Acknowledgements

This book was written in fits and starts, from the seed of an idea that took root sometime in the early 1990's to what now finds its way to your hands and eyes.

It's been a winding, rocky road to get to where I am better able to hear and follow the wisdom that brings true inner strength and resilience, and it has brought me many teachers. Some were accidental — I learned from them how I *didn't* want to be — and others were chosen, inspiring me with their unique combination of love, compassion, faith and wisdom. I'm going to name some names and I'm sure I'll forget a few; some are people who no longer are in my life but had a deep impact through their unfailing insistence that I write a book to share what I've learned with others.

First I want to thank my parents, Robert and Barbara Rosen (of blessed memory). They taught me to think for myself and do good in the world. They provided a deep love that made me feel safe and secure, even when we were at odds with one another. I am proud to be the product of their union. Sadly, my mother died while I was editing this book and never had a chance to read it or hold a copy. I am grateful that I showed her the cover proof on one of our last visits, and watched her rejoice in the fact that I'd chosen to use my full name, a preference she had strongly voiced when asked. You won, Mom! And now you get to rest.

One of my best teachers is my husband, Rick Lashinsky, who enables me daily to know what unconditional love feels like. He has become a sure and solid ground beneath my feet without ever making me feel tied down. His loving devotion, ability to help me laugh at myself and great taste in music give me much to be grateful for.

My life is cradled in a tightly woven fabric of friends, from high school and college on through my years of work in the healing arts and spiritual studies. A huge hug goes out to these kindred souls: Diane, Lisa, Emily, Ellen, Michele, Naomi, Gailann, Bonnie, Suzannah, Elizabeth, Susan H., Judy M., Judy R., Loretta, Florence, Annie, Claudia, Nurit, and the New Paltz *No Wrong Notes* music makers. Thank you for loving me, laughing with me, cradling me through the rough times and celebrating the joys of life with me. May we all end up together in heaven, singing, dancing and eating exquisite chocolate.

I've never birthed a child, but bringing this book to life has been a long and sometimes painful process. I was lucky to have many midwives and doulas to hold my hand, rub my back and ease the way. To my generous first readers and editors, Kirsten Carle, Matthew David O'Grady, Claudia Forest, Shonda Taylor and Fran Bartkowski; your support, encouragement and belief in this project helped me bring greater clarity of voice and vision to it.

To Byron Katie and her colleagues, for so graciously allowing me to share her teaching and for editing Chapter 4 so that it most accurately portrays The Work.

To all of the clients I've been blessed to work with over 25 years of massage and Kabbalistic healing sessions, Reiki and self-care classes: you trust me with your bodies, your stories and your souls. I am grateful to touch whatever part of your life I can, and to learn and grow with you.

To Ann Bird, an extraordinary therapist, who with great compassion, wisdom and humor helped me learn what it really means to grow up.

To my Kabbalistic Healing teacher, Jason Shulman. Thank you for allowing me to share one of your beautiful nigguns, but most of all for making Kabbalah and the Tree of Life come alive for me. Your words and brilliance opened me to so much healing, and gave me one of my favorite touchstone phrases, "Interesting if true."

Recommended Resources

Books

Kabbalistic Healing, A Path to an Awakened Soul (Jason Shulman, Inner Traditions, 2004).

The Instruction Manual for Receiving God (Jason Shulman, Sounds True, Inc. 2006).

Loving What Is, Four Questions That Can Change Your Life (Byron Katie, Three Rivers Press, 2002).

I Need Your Love – Is That True? (Byron Katie, Harmony Books, 2005).

Oracles

Motherpeace: A Way to the Goddess Through Myth, Art and Tarot and accompanying card deck (Vicki Noble, HarperSanFrancisco, 1983).

The Kabbalah Deck (Edward Hoffman, Chronicle Books, 2000).

The Book of Runes (Ralph Blum, St. Martin's Press, 1993).

The Original Angel Cards (Kathy Tyler and Joy Drake, Allegro Corporation, 2006).

Websites

www.heartofselfcare.com: My main website for info on SpiritWise Wellness programs, Radical Self-Care classes, Mindful Way meditation instruction and individual sessions. Contact me at sharon@heartofselfcare.com about speaking to your group or organization, or presenting a workshop based on the concepts in *Crazy World, Peaceful Heart.*

www.kabbalah.org: The work of Jason Shulman and A Society of Souls

www.thework.com: The Work of Byron Katie

ABOUT THE AUTHOR

Sharon Helene Rosen was born to explore, integrate and share an array of the world's most effective healing tools. Always drawn to alternative approaches, her interest was heightened by a desire to heal her own physical and emotional issues that began in high school.

This quest led her to become certified as a massage therapist, Reiki master/teacher, kabbalistic healer, wellness coach and meditation instructor, with a wide range of healing modalities gathered along the way. Her focus in every encounter is on evoking the innate ability we each have to hold stress-in-balance and thrive in the midst of a crazy, busy life. Clients value her deep listening, comforting, non-judgmental manner, intuitive insights and comprehensive approach to holistic healing.

For 25 years Sharon has led thousands of clients from overwhelm, frustration and pain to clarity, ease and relief. As they release physical and emotional discomforts, they find they can be more productive, experience better relationships and get more joy out of life.

Sharon has had articles published in magazines including *Yoga Journal, Relevant Times* and *Holistic Living*, and is a featured author at *ezinearticles.com* and *selfgrowth.com*. This is her first book.

CPSIA information can be obtained at www.ICGtesting.com
Printed in the USA
BVOW032317061112

304833BV00001B/1/P